—— Family Scrapbook

A Wartime Childhood

Family Scrapbook

A Wartime Childhood

Rebecca Hunter with Angela Downey

Evans

Family Scrapbook: A Wartime Childhood

Published by in 2005 by Evans Brothers Limited
2A Portman Mansions
Chiltern St
London W1U 6NR

British Cataloguing in Publication Data
Hunter, Rebecca
Grandma's War
1.War– Great Britain – History – 20th century – Juvenile literature
2.Children – Great Britain -Social conditions – 20th century – Juvenile literature
3.Great Britain – Social life and customs – 20th century – Juvenile literature
4.Great Britain – History – 20th century – Juvenile literature
I. Title
II. Downey, Angela
941'.084

ISBN 0 237 52901 7
13 digit ISBN (from January 2007) 978 0 237 52901 7

Acknowledgements
Planning and production by Discovery Books Limited
Edited by Rebecca Hunter
Designed by Ian Winton
Commissioned photography by Alex Ramsay
Illustrations by Stuart Lafford

The publisher would like to thank Angela Downey for her kind help in the preparation of this book.

For permission to reproduce copyright material, the author and publishers gratefully acknowledge the following:
The Advertising Archives 23 (bottom); AKG London 10 (top); London Borough of Wandsworth cover (top right),
19 (bottom); The Hulton Getty Picture Collection Library 10 (bottom) 25, 26; The Imperial War Museum 8 (bottom),
9 (top), 13 (top), 15, 16, 17, 19 (top), 20, 22, 23 (top), 24; The London Borough of Lambeth Archives Department 7;
Peter Newark's Pictures cover (left), 11, 12, 18 (bottom); The Robert Opie Collection cover (top), 8 (top).

'I was born in 1937.'

My name is Angela and I am a grandmother. I have six grandchildren. Here I am with Adam who is thirteen, Jack who is eleven and Luke who is five.

When I was young, my family lived in Clapham, London. The picture above shows what Clapham looked like when I was young.

My dad worked for the post office and my mum was a housewife. I had two older brothers called Cecil and John.

I was born in 1937 before the **Second World War**. Many things changed after the war started. I am going to tell you about what life was like during the war.

'We all had gas masks.'

The war started in Europe in 1939. We were all given rubber gas masks in case poison gas was dropped from aeroplanes. Children's gas masks were made in bright colours to make them less frightening.

THIS SPECIAL RESPIRATOR FOR A SMALL CHILD IS GOVERNMENT PROPERTY. ANY PERSON WHO HAS IT IN HIS POSSESSION IS RESPONSIBLE IN LAW FOR USING CARE TO KEEP IT IN GOOD CONDITION. IT IS TO BE RETURNED TO THE LOCAL AUTHORITY IN WHOSE AREA THE POSSESSOR MAY BE AT ANY TIME, EITHER ON REQUEST OR WHEN NO LONGER REQUIRED.

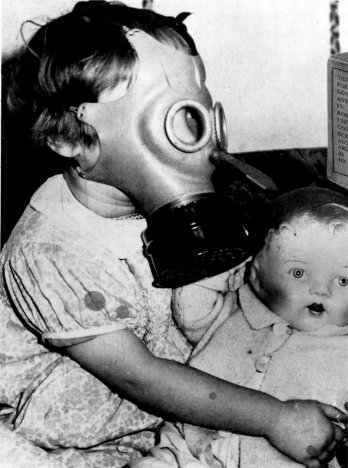

It was very dangerous living in London. Air-raid sirens made a terrible wailing noise when the enemy planes were coming to drop bombs. You had to find shelter, quickly.

Some of our
neighbours built
**Anderson bomb
shelters** like this in
their gardens, but
we sheltered in
Clapham Common
underground
station.

Small children were put in
siren suits to keep them
warm in the shelters. This
is me wearing one.

'Put out that light!'

Air raids took place at night. My brothers helped my mum put up big black curtains over the windows so enemy planes couldn't see the lights from our house.

ARP wardens walked up and down our street checking that no light could be seen outside. If they saw even a chink of light through the curtains they shouted, 'Put out that light!'

The picture on the left shows a warden's post made out of sandbags. Sandbags were used as protection during air raids.

It was dangerous to be outside during the **blackout** because there were no street lights and cars drove about without lights on.

White lines were painted on kerbs and steps to help people find their way, but there were still lots of accidents.

Pat Keely

UNTIL YOUR EYES
GET USED TO
THE DARKNESS,
TAKE IT EASY

LOOK OUT IN THE BLACKOUT

'I was evacuated to Devon.'

In 1940 my father was **called up** and sent with the army to fight abroad. The government said that children in cities should be **evacuated** to the countryside, which was safer.

LEAVE THIS TO US SONMY — <u>YOU</u> OUGHT TO BE OUT OF LONDON

MINISTRY OF HEALTH EVACUATION SCHEME

My two brothers were sent to Yorkshire. I was evacuated in 1941 to a small village in Devon called Clyst St Mary. My mum came with me.

The train was packed with other children. We all had labels around our necks with our names, ages and where we were going. We carried our gas masks in a box strung around our necks. I took my favourite doll with me too, in case she got broken in the bombing.

'I went to the local school.'

When we got to Clyst St Mary I met the family who were going to **foster** me and said goodbye to my mum. I would see her only once a year for the next three years. I felt very homesick.

This is how Clyst St Mary looked then. It was very quiet compared to London.

I went to the local village school. The school kept daily records of events. Here are the records for two weeks in March 1942 showing the arrival of an evacuee and the dates when the gas masks were checked.

Exeter was our nearest big town. Sometimes I went shopping there with my foster mum.

'Everyone joined in with war work.'

Life was hard for everyone during the war. Many men had to leave their jobs and families to join the armed forces. Others did war work in factories. My foster dad worked in a factory in Exeter, building and repairing aircraft.

Any men who were not involved in the fighting were encouraged to help in the war effort by joining the **Local Defence Volunteers**.

To start with they had no uniforms or weapons. They looked quite funny parading in their ordinary clothes with broom handles instead of rifles!

The boy scouts in our village used to collect **salvage**. Old saucepans, kettles, tin cans and iron railings could be made into new war weapons.

Farmers still needed help to grow food on the farm so women were encouraged to join the Women's Land Army. Many young women came down to the countryside to work on the farms.

'London was bombed in the Blitz.'

My mum had stayed in London to work as a ticket collector for London Transport.

Enjoy your War Work

Look out in the blackout

GOOD PAY · FREE UNIFORM AND AN INTERESTING JOB

LONDON NEEDS MORE WOMEN BUS AND TRAM CONDUCTORS

SEE LARGE POSTERS FOR PARTICULARS

She sent me letters telling me how hard life was in London. She told me food was in very short supply because ships carrying supplies could not get through.

RATION BOOK

Many foods were **rationed**. Everyone had a ration book with coupons showing how much they could buy each week.

People were encouraged to grow their own vegetables. Clapham Common (above), where we used to play, was turned into allotments!

Many areas in London were badly damaged by bombs during the **Blitz**. This is Balham High Road after a bombing raid.

'We played in the fields.'

Life in Devon was easier than in London. Although food was rationed we ate quite well. I helped my foster dad in the garden where we grew our own vegetables. Country life was a new experience for me and I enjoyed visiting a farm for the first time and playing in the fields at hay-making time.

In 1942 I heard that my dad had been killed fighting overseas. I hadn't seen him for two years and now I would never see him again.

This made me very worried about my mum. Here is a letter I sent her telling her what I was doing and how I felt. I called myself Ann when I was a child.

Plymt St Mary

My Dea Mum
Here is a line hoping you are a Lot Better And will be out of Hospital soon I have A new school Teatcher I have been good At school and never Had the cane once I went in Exeter Last Thurs day with Pegg and gwen To get a pair of Sand als give My Love to Cecil ALL My Love MuMy. God BLess You and keep you from the bombs Love Ann

'We loved the American soldiers.'

Parachutes and **armaments** were made in Exeter. This made the city a target for enemy attack. In 1942 the city was badly bombed. The boards in this picture show where the shops used to stand. Fortunately the cathedral was not damaged.

America was one of our **allies** in the war and many American soldiers arrived in the country to help fight. The boys in our village loved to talk to them and try on their uniforms!

Everyone loved the American soldiers because they could get things like chocolate and cigarettes that were in short supply. They would drive through the village in their trucks, throwing sweets and chewing gum out of the windows to the children. I had never tasted chewing gum before!

'I returned home for Christmas.'

My brothers and I finally returned home to London in time for Christmas 1944, shortly before the war ended.

London had been badly hit by a new type of flying bomb - the V1, or doodlebug. It made a droning noise as it travelled. When the noise stopped, you knew the bomb was dropping down to explode.

This picture shows Clapham after it was hit by a doodlebug.

Later came an even more terrifying weapon - the V2 rocket - which gave no warning at all. You couldn't hear them coming until it was too late. This picture shows one, about to be launched on London.

My brothers and I enjoyed playing on bomb sites. We made dens and hiding places in the ruins and searched for pieces of **shrapnel** amongst the rubble. I broke my arm falling off a homemade swing!

'Parties went on for days.'

The war in Europe finally ended in May 1945, although the war against Japan went on until August. Victory in Europe, or VE Day as it became known, was declared and we all celebrated.

DAILY EXPRESS

WAR OVER IN GERMANY, HOLLAND AND DENMARK

GERMANS SURRENDER INSIDE MONTY'S TENT

They argued, they wept, they went and lunched— but said 'Yes' at last

THE MAP CONVINCED THEM

THE TERMS WITH NO ARGUMENT

RUNDSTEDT TELLS

Why we lost

COLD, RUTHLESS

DRINK ORGY ENDS REICH

Doenitz off to Norway

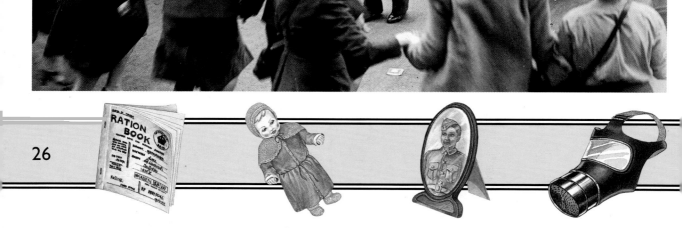

Street parties, with bonfires, fireworks and music went on all over the country for many days. The local council gave a party in our school to celebrate. There were many decorations and flags, and food like jelly and ice cream that we hadn't tasted for a very long time.

Here is a photo of that party. I am sitting on the right.

'After the war.'

Last year I returned to the village of Clyst St Mary to show my husband where I had spent most of the war.

A lady in the village found this photograph showing me (holding the dog) which was taken after the war had finished.

I lived through some exciting times during the war but I will never forget how many people lost their lives. I certainly wouldn't want my grandchildren to live through a war like that.

GLOSSARY

air raids Attacks from the air by aeroplanes, rockets and bombs.

allies Britain, the USA and the USSR fought together as allies against Germany, Italy and Japan during the war.

Anderson shelter An outdoor air raid shelter made of corrugated steel.

armaments Military weapons and equipment.

ARP wardens Air Raid Precautions (ARP) wardens were responsible for checking air raid shelters and enforcing the blackout.

blackout Making sure no light was visible from houses or streets so that towns were invisible from the air.

Blitz The 'Blitzkrieg' or 'Blitz' was the heavy night-time bombing of British cities in 1940 and 1941.

call up An order from the government to join the armed forces.

evacuate To remove people from a dangerous place to a safer one.

foster To look after children that are not your own.

Local Defence Volunteers A voluntary group of men who wanted to help defend their towns and villages if there was an invasion by the Germans.

rationing Limiting the amount of food and clothing that a person is allowed to buy.

salvage To re-use goods and materials for other purposes.

Second World War A war fought around the world between 1939 and 1945. Germany, Italy, Japan and their allies were on one side and Britain, the United States, the Soviet Union and their allies were on the other.

shrapnel Small fragments of bombs.

OTHER BOOKS TO READ

Other books about twentieth-century history for younger readers published by Evans include:

INDEX